HOW

a

BIBLE
PRINCESS

How to Be a Bible Princess

Catherine Mackenzie

CF4·K

Dedication:
For all my nieces

10 9 8 7 6 5 4 3 2 1

© Copyright 2012 Christian Focus Publications
ISBN: 978-1-84550-825-8

Published in 2012 by
Christian Focus Publications,
Geanies House, Fearn, Tain, Ross-shire, IV20 1TW, U.K.

Cover design by Daniel van Straaten
Illustrations by Jeff Anderson
Printed and bound by Nørhaven, Denmark

CONTENTS

WHaT iS a PRiNCeSS?

hat would you do if you woke up one morning to discover that overnight you'd become a princess?

Would you:-

a) Jump out of bed and rush to your super-sized wardrobe chock-a-block with bling! Try on Monday morning's tiara and send off an order for some diamond-studded shoes to match?

b) Shout 'Off with their heads' – just for the practice?

c) Check on all the handsome princes out there?

d) Curtsey to your mother and then write a list, checking it twice, about all the really good causes you're going to support?

If you answered a) – watch out for a revolution; your crazy spending habits will not make your subjects like you.

If you answered b) – watch out for a revolution; chopping off people's heads will not make your subjects like you. Not at all.

If you answered c) – Watch out for a revolution; the ugly princes might be offended.

If you answered d) – you're safe! Phew! You're such a nice all-round good-girl princess that all the revolutionaries will just love you!

With all that talk of revolutions, perhaps you've changed your mind about being a princess. It might not be the best career choice. Perhaps being a princess is not all it's cracked up to be. Is the life of a princess all about jewels and dances? Could it be about wars and battles too?

Being a princess is certainly a life of privilege and power – for some it is a great life. But the princesses we're going to read about don't quite fit the glitzy-ditzy image that some imagine is the life of a royal princess. In this book we have princesses who showed just as much bravery as warriors – yet they didn't carry swords. We also have princesses who were sharp thinkers – women who made wise decisions. And we've got quite a few princesses who did the wisest thing of all - trust in God.

You see, all these princesses are from the Bible – and that is something that should make you sit up and take notice. God has put these women in his Word for a reason – and you need to find out why.

But not all the princesses in this book are heroines. Some of the royal ladies in the Bible were lean mean killing machines – the bad princesses of the Bible. Yeah, watch out for those girls! One of them comes to a particularly grizzly end – not good if you're feeling a bit squeamish.

'Hang on a second,' I hear you say. 'This book is How to be a Bible princess. What do you mean exactly? Can I be a princess?'

Good question. Here's the deal. Unless you're born in a royal family, or marry a prince, you're not going to be a princess. But you can join a royal family – THE royal family – God's family. Being part of God's family is not about birth or status or if you've got a crown or two in your cupboard. It's not about what you look like, or about being in charge. It's not even about being the nicest, most organised, generous person around. Being a Bible princess is about being part of the true royal family that has God the Father, God the Son and God the Holy Spirit at its centre. It's a family that anyone can enter into if they trust in the Lord Jesus Christ to save them from their sins.

If you trust in Jesus to save you from sin you are something even better than a worldly princess, you are a child of God. Your creator has made you – a girl – and he has saved you – a sinner. And one day you will be perfect, privileged and beautiful beyond imagination. That's what being a Bible princess is all about. It's really about being a child of God. A sinner saved by God's grace. When you trust in Jesus, the wrong things that you've done are wiped away because of God's love, power and wonderful mercy. Read on and find out more about how you can be part of the true royal family ... God's family!

PhaRaoh'S DaUGhteR

What would you do if you were going for a bath and you discovered an unknown baby in a shopping basket floating in the water? Would you: -

a) Stop and rub your eyes and decide you're seeing things?

b) Scream – loud and long?

c) Go 'oohs a pwetty baby goo goo gaa gaaa,' in delight?

Well, it's a good job for one little Hebrew baby that a certain Egyptian princess was a c).

But why was this baby floating in a basket on the River Nile. What is going on? Let's find out ...

When the Egyptian princess saw the floating basket, she was curious. Princesses are just as nosy as everybody else, so she sent one of her maids down into the water to lift it out. The frantic squawking from inside would soon have told the princess and her maids that it was ...

'A baby,' said one girl.

'A boy,' said another.

'It's a Hebrew,' one of the maids whispered.

Now, the supreme ruler of all Egypt, the great Pharaoh himself, didn't like the Hebrews. No one disobeyed the Pharaoh. His subjects called him all sorts of things like – Your Greatness, Your Excellency, the most wonderful ruler in the entire world who is the strongest, most handsome and super intelligent. You know the kind of thing we're talking about? On a good day the princess was sometimes allowed to call him Dad.

But as the princess's dad was the driving force behind the nationwide scheme to destroy the Hebrew people, having a Hebrew baby as a pet was not a good idea. Even princesses have to obey supreme rulers. This was going to be tricky.

Just then the real heroine of the story jumped out of a clump of bulrushes. She wasn't a princess; she wasn't even an Egyptian. She was, in fact, the baby's sister and her name was Miriam.

She didn't tell the princess who she was. Miriam knew who she was dealing with. Miriam knew that she had to be careful. Her baby brother's life depended on it because Pharaoh had ordered that all the Hebrew boys should be killed at birth.

Jochabed, Miriam's mum, had hidden her baby son for as long as she could, but now that he was getting bigger and noisier, it was much harder. So Jochabed had made a little waterproof boat out of bulrushes and set her child adrift on the river. It wasn't as though he would be left totally alone because his big sister would be keeping an eye on him.

That had been the plan ... but when the princess came along Miriam had another idea – and oh, it was a good one. It was a GOD one.

Miriam approached the princess respectfully. Perhaps she said something like this ... 'What a beautiful little boy. Would you like me to go and arrange for one of the Hebrew women to be his nurse for you? She can do all the dirty work and you can have the baby to come and play with you at the palace. That would be nice, wouldn't it?'

This plan was brilliant. Miriam and her family would get the best of both worlds. The princess would employ Jochabed as the baby's nurse; they would get to keep the baby and the Princess would become their friend. Miriam's baby brother

would be safe – and they would get paid for doing what they had been doing anyway!

The princess also got the best of both worlds – no dirty baby bottoms to wipe and a little baby to play with whenever she wanted. The princess took up Miriam's suggestion. She chose a name for him – Moses. This means 'out of the water'. Now that's quite clever.

The baby was the one who really got the best of both worlds. He was nurtured and protected by the family that God had given him. He wasn't thrown into the River Nile to drown and he grew up as part of Pharaoh's household. Moses learned the truth of God's Word from his real family, which was great. The baby in the basket grew up to be the leader of God's people and fulfil God's plan for the Hebrews.

Read the story of Miriam and Moses in Exodus chapter 2.

PRiNCeSS TiPS

Who is the real 'Bible Princess' in this story? Here's a clue – it's not the one with the crown on her head. It's the one hiding in the bulrushes. That's right – Miriam. So what can you learn from her story that will help you please God? Miriam did what was right in God's eyes. She obeyed God and as a result she saved a life. Life is a gift from God. God gives life from even before someone is born, right up to the moment a person dies.

But who is the real hero of this story? It's God. It was his plan to save Moses. He prompted Jochabed and Miriam to do what they did. He arranged it so that Pharaoh's daughter came along when she did. And it was God who made sure she was in a 'aren't babies gorgeous' sort of mood.

Think about Jesus

What is God's family and how do you join it? Being in God's family is not about having Mary and Joseph as your parents. That's not the family we are talking about.

Mary and Joseph were part of Jesus' earthly family, but his real Father was God. It was God's Holy Spirit who overshadowed Mary and gave her a child in her womb. God also provided Mary with a husband, and Jesus with an earthly father to provide for his daily needs. His name was Joseph. After Jesus was born, Mary and Joseph had other children of their own, brothers and sisters for Jesus. But remember, God's family is a different family; it's not about blood relations.

When Jesus grew up and started his public ministry he preached and performed miracles in order to show people who God was. One day when Jesus was speaking with his followers someone came to tell him that his mother and brothers were waiting for him outside. Jesus then said something strange. 'Who are my mother and brothers?' He pointed to his followers and said, 'Here are my mother and brothers.' Jesus wasn't being disrespectful to Mary or his family. What he was saying was that his real family were those who loved and trusted God. For you to be a child of God – part of the heavenly royal family – you need to be a follower of Jesus.

How can you be a follower of Jesus? You need to recognise that you are a sinner. What's a sinner? The Bible tells us that, '*All have sinned and fallen short of the glory of God*' (Romans 3:23). We all do what displeases God and that's called sin.

You need to recognise that Jesus is the one and only Saviour. Only he can give you salvation.

What's salvation? Well, the Bible tells us that '*For God so loved the world that he gave his one and only Son, that whoever believes in him shall not perish but have eternal life*' (John 3:16). It also tells us to '*Believe in the Lord Jesus and you will be saved*' (Acts 16:31).

Salvation is to be saved from the punishment of sin. Sinners are saved by trusting in Jesus and what he did on the cross. Sinners deserve punishment, but are saved from this and given eternal life through the grace of God. It is Jesus' death that takes dirty, lost, broken sinners and changes them to being part of God's family. You must understand that you are a sinner, that you need to be saved and that Jesus is the only one who can do this.

Read more: You can read about Jesus' early life in Luke chapter 2.

ABigaiL: Beauty and Brains

What would you do if you were married to an idiot? Let's stop right there because I hope that all of you, if you get married, will get married to someone who is wise and godly. Right? Right! However, the woman in this story was, unfortunately, married to an idiot. His name was Nabal and that meant fool – so fool by name fool by nature.

Let's start again. What would you do if you had an idiotic husband (which you won't) and one day he drops you in a whole lot of trouble with a tribe of fearsome warriors? But it's not just you; it's you and everyone who works for your husband. You may even be in danger of losing your life. What would you do? Would you ...

a) Pack your bags and head for the nearest budget airline, with all your credit cards, jewellery, his piggy bank, the larder, your clothes, his watches and the cat?

b) Brush up on your Kung Fu boxing moves, barricade the windows, lock all the doors and hide under the bed with your knitting needles?

c) Decide to meet the danger head on, while taking the fearsome warriors really good food – and lots of it?

This is not a good situation to be in, is it? I wouldn't want to make that decision. I wonder what you would chose?

If you picked a), well, I'm not so sure you're the kind of girl who is good in a crisis. Making a run for it might be considered a sensible option, but leaving your other half behind is not the Bible way. Read Exodus 20:14 and Ephesians 5:22-33. This shows us how wives should treat their husbands. And taking the piggy bank! Well – really – that's just mean and it breaks another of God's commandments.

If you picked b), well, hang on a second! This is a tribe of fearsome warriors we're talking about. Barricaded windows and locked doors won't stop them. And knitting needles? Are you mad? They might be OK for making a cardigan but they're going to be useless against men carrying swords and spears.

If you picked c), well, I hope you're a better cook than me. But it's the right answer, so go to the top of the class.

Now sit back, relax, and find out about our next princess. She's called Abigail. When we first meet her in 1 Samuel 25, she is not a princess. She is, however, described as discerning and beautiful. The idiot husband is described as harsh and badly behaved. Let's find out what happened ...

This story starts with a king, King David. At this point in David's life he wasn't officially recognised as the King of Israel, but he had been anointed as King by the prophet Samuel. As King Saul had displeased God, David was chosen to replace him – even though he was the youngest of his brothers and just a shepherd boy. Over time he proved himself to be a courageous and godly young man and Saul hated him for it. When David defeated the giant Goliath with a sling shot and God's power, the people loved him and praised him more than they praised Saul. David had to flee for his life, because Saul's jealousy got out of control.

David and his band of warriors had to flee here and there all over the country. They were in and out of deserts and wildernesses, even taking refuge in other countries. Just after the prophet Samuel died, David and his men were in the wilderness of Paran. In that area there was a man who was very rich – Nabal (yes, the idiot). He had thousands of sheep and goats and it was shearing time. That's the time when all the sheep are gathered in to have their fleeces removed. The wool is then made ready to be sold at market.

Throughout the weeks when Nabal's workers had been gathering in the animals, David and his men had let them get on with their work. Sometimes they had even protected them from bandits who might have stolen their flocks.

David could easily have behaved differently. He and his men were on the run and in desperate need of food. Nabal wouldn't have missed a sheep or two, but David had left the man's flocks alone.

Now that the time for shearing had come, a great feast was planned and David heard about it. He sent ten of his young men to speak to Nabal.

The messengers greeted Nabal with a message from David, 'Peace to you and to your house. We have heard that you have the shearers at your farm and, since we have been with your shepherds all this time and have done them no harm, let us find favour in your eyes on your feast day. Please give whatever you have at hand to your servants and to David.'

The messengers waited for Nabal's reply and this is what it was ...

'Who is David? Who is this Son of Jesse? I've heard that there are many servants these days running away from their masters. Shall I take my bread and my water, and my meat that I have killed for my shearers and give it to men who come from I know not where?'

Well, that was just rude!

So the young men turned away, came back to David and told him everything that Nabal had said.

David was furious. 'Every man strap on his sword!' he yelled. And about four hundred fighting men got ready to follow him. David and his men made ready for war and set off towards Nabal's farm.

However, one of Nabal's servants decided that his mistress needed to hear what was going on. Wise move. Abigail was obviously the smart one in that household.

The servant ran up to his mistress and spilt the beans, 'David sent messengers to greet our master and he lost his temper with them. Yet David's men have been very good to us, and we've suffered no harm all the time they have been here. They didn't steal from us, and even protected us like a wall during the day and during the night. What do you think we should do? Our master and this whole household will come to much harm because of what he has done and there is no one who can speak to our master because he is such a worthless man.'

Abigail didn't waste any time. She hurried and took two hundred loaves and two large containers of wine and five sheep butchered and ready for eating. She also took parched grain and clusters of raisins and cakes of figs. There was enough to feed a small army – because that was what was coming over the hill ready to cut her household to pieces if she didn't do something to stop them.

Abigail knew that she couldn't fight with a sword; she wasn't a warrior. She also knew that she couldn't run and leave behind her husband and all the people who depended on her. That was just not acceptable. The only thing she could do was bring a message of peace.

Abigail put all the provisions onto donkeys and headed into the wilderness to confront David. She decided wisely not to tell her husband what she was up to. Who knows what he would have done if she had, probably something foolish.

As Abigail and the shepherds approached the mountain, David and his men came towards her.

David was grumbling as he made his way towards the farm. 'Surely it's been a complete waste of my time guarding all that this fellow, Nabal, has in this wilderness. Nothing was taken from his belongings thanks to us. Yet he has returned to me evil for good. By morning there won't be even one male alive of all who belong to Nabal.'

Abigail heard David's complaints and fell on the ground before him. She begged him to listen to her, ignore Nabal, and accept the gifts she had brought. Abigail pleaded with David, 'The LORD will make you a sure house because you are fighting the battles of the LORD and evil shall not be found in you as long as you live. If men rise up to pursue you and seek your life, you shall be bound in the bundle of the living in the care of the LORD your God. And the lives of your enemies, he shall sling out as from the hollow of a sling.'

'And when the LORD has appointed you prince over Israel, you shall have no grief or pangs of conscience for having shed blood without cause. When the LORD has dealt well with you, then remember me, your servant.'

David replied, 'Blessed be the LORD, the God of Israel who sent you this day to meet me! Blessed be your discretion and blessed be you who have kept me from avenging myself with my own hand. Unless you had hurried and come to meet me, truly by morning there would not have been left one male in Nabal's household.'

David accepted Abigail's gifts and said to her, 'Go in peace. See I have obeyed your voice and granted your petition.'

The next day, when Abigail told Nabal what had happened, he got such a shock that he collapsed as if dead. Ten days later, in fact, he was dead. When David heard this, he thanked God and asked Abigail to consider being his wife. Abigail agreed at once. Again, she didn't waste any time. Taking five of her women she mounted a donkey and set off to become the wife of the future King of Israel.

You can read the story about Abigail in
1 Samuel 25.

PRiNCeSS TiPS

Before Abigail became a princess, people knew how special she was. She was beautiful, but beauty comes and goes, and different people think that different things are beautiful or pretty. The most important thing about Abigail, was that she was discerning. That's another word for wise.

Wisdom is more than just being clever. Lots of people can answer difficult questions in a maths test – but they ignore God. Those people are foolish and not wise. You might get someone who isn't very clever and fails every spelling test that there is, but who trusts in God and follows his ways. That person is wise.

Abigail's wisdom came from God. True wisdom is a gift from God and he is willing to give it to anyone who asks. (See James 1:5)

Think about Jesus

What are you like? If you were to pick some words that sum you up, what would they be? Fun, quiet, noisy, busy? These words are called characteristics. They sum up what you are like. Abigail's characteristic was discernment or wisdom. Wisdom is a characteristic of Jesus Christ. That is what he is like. He is wise.

Jesus astonished people with his knowledge and understanding, even as a child. When he was twelve, he accompanied his parents to the temple in Jerusalem, but his parents lost track of where he was. Mary and Joseph only realised he was missing after they had begun their journey back home. They searched for him for days and eventually found him in the temple. Jesus had been there talking about God with the priests. The priests were astonished at his wisdom. It was amazing to find such knowledge in a young boy.

Luke 2:52 says Jesus grew in wisdom and stature, and in favour with God and man. This verse shows that, as well as being a normal boy and growing out of all his coats and sandals, Jesus also gained more and more wisdom as he matured. God saw this and was pleased with his one and only Son.

But did you know that God was also angry with the Son that he loved? Does that sound strange?

When Jesus died on the cross he suffered greatly, he was hurt and bleeding. But his spirit was hurting too. This was harder. He was taking God's punishment for sin. That was the only way for sinners to be made right with God and be given eternal life. God's anger had to be poured on his Son. Jesus died willingly and took sin on himself, so that sinners could have his goodness instead. Jesus took the punishment he did not deserve, so that sinners could have everlasting life that they did not deserve. God poured out his anger on Jesus, but then he exalted his Son by raising him from the dead. And one day every knee shall bow and every tongue confess that Jesus Christ is Lord.

Read more: The story of the resurrection of Jesus can be read in John 20.

JehoSheba to the Rescue

Now, sometimes in history you have people who do really important things, but not much is said about them. This is true of the princess, Jehosheba. What she did was amazing – her bravery and quick thinking enabled her to pull off a most important rescue. You don't hear much about her in the Bible, however. Let's start though with another question ...

Imagine you're in the middle of a revolution. There are riots in the streets. Nowhere is safe. It looks as though the country is going to be taken over by an evil dictator. There is one person still alive who might in time be able to turn things around. But it could be years before he is able to do this. He's the heir to the throne and he is only a few months old. He is being held captive in the palace and needs to be rescued. What do you think is the best way to accomplish this? Would you ...

a) Get your own private army, tanks, missiles, anti-aircraft guns and lasers – turn them on the palace and let rip?

b) Start digging a tunnel?

c) Get someone inside the palace itself to do the job?

Well, if you answered a) – that might make a great movie, but how would you be sure the baby would get out alive? You'd kill the enemy for sure, but you might also kill the person you're trying to rescue.

If you answered b) – you've been watching too many movies. Digging tunnels doesn't often work and they take ages. In any case, you'd probably end up in the toilets when you'd meant to dig your way into the nursery. Not a good idea.

If c) was your answer – well done! A brilliant strategy. And one that was used to good effect in the story we're going to read now.

But first we need to look at a little bit of history.

Things in Israel had been deteriorating ever since the death of King David. The nation had split in two. Both countries had their own royal families and armies. One country was called Judah and the other Israel. Although the original kingdom was divided, both countries sometimes joined forces to fight a common enemy. But they also fought each other from time to time.

Sadly, the kings of Judah and Israel had abandoned the worship of the one true God, to worship idols instead. There was the odd exception, such as Jehoshephat and Jehu who were known to follow God. But they also made mistakes and sinned against the LORD.

Only some of God's prophets like Micaiah, Elijah and Elisha stood up against the rot that was setting in.

When King Ahaziah took the throne of Judah he was a young man of twenty-two, but his reign was very short. It only lasted for a year. Now, his mother's name was Athaliah, but it might have been better if she'd been named Trouble, Disaster or Rotten-cheating-scoundrel. She is one of the princesses in the Bible that we don't want to be like.

When Ahaziah died, his mother, Athaliah, decided that it would be a good idea to destroy all the royal family. She wanted to have every possible successor to Ahaziah's throne disposed of. Some of the young men she murdered would have been her own relatives, even grandchildren. What a despicably evil woman she was.

However, one of those princes was going to be rescued by Jehosheba. She was a sister of King Ahaziah and a princess of Judah. She knew that she had to protect the royal family by rescuing at least one of her brother's descendants. There had to be an heir to the throne who would one day defeat Athaliah.

The prince who was to be saved was called Joash. He must have been young, as he still had to have a nurse to look after him. Jehosheba, his aunt, hatched a plot to rescue this little boy.

Jehosheba knew the layout of the palace rooms. She knew where the young princes were gathered. She had access to the palace and could come and go as she pleased. So that's how this particular princess managed to sneak in and steal away young Joash and his nurse.

Once he had been rescued, how did Jehosheba keep him safe? She had to hide him somewhere, somewhere that Athaliah never went. As Athaliah did not worship the one true God, the safest place for the young prince was in the temple.

Jehosheba was actually married to the priest, Jehoida, and it was to him that she handed over the young prince for hiding.

For six years Athaliah ruled the land and, when the young prince, Joash, was just over seven years old, Jehoida, the priest sent for the commanders and guards and had them brought to the temple of the Lord. He showed them the late king's son and commanded them all to station themselves around the young King Joash with their weapons on the Lord's day.

'You are to stay with him wherever he goes,' Jehoida ordered.

The commanders and guards did just as Jehoida commanded. They surrounded Joash near the altar. Every side was covered. Jehoiada crowned Joash and anointed him.

The people clapped their hands and shouted, 'Long live the king!'

When Athaliah heard all the noise she marched straight into the temple. There, standing by the pillar was the young King Joash – her own grandson, the one she had thought murdered on that night six years ago. Trumpets sounded and there was great rejoicing, but all Athaliah could do was tear her clothes and yell at the top of her voice, 'Treason! Treason!'

Jehoida ordered that Athaliah and anyone who supported her should be siezed. They were to be taken out of the temple and put to death.

Athaliah must have tried to make a run for it, but the commanders of the troops caught up with her just at the place where the horses entered the palace grounds and there she was put to death.

Jehoida then made a special promise between God, the new king and the people – that they would be the LORD's people. Then everyone went

to the temple of Baal – the false god that Athaliah had followed – and they tore it down until it was all smashed to pieces.

Joash was taken in great style to the palace to take his rightful place on the royal throne.

You can read the story of Jehosheba in 2 Kings 11.

PRiNCeSS TiPS

Brave women are so inspiring. Jehosheba put her life on the line to save someone else. You can show courage in your own life by standing up for the kingdom of God. When people make fun of you for doing the 'Christian' thing, ignore them. Be inspiring. Honour God.

ThiNK aBoUt JeSUS

If you look at Jesus' family tree in Matthew 1 you will be able to trace Jesus' ancestry right back to King David. But Joash is missed out. Why is that? Well, it may be because Joash was related to the wicked king, Ahab, and his wife Jezebel. But it also could be because there is a sad ending to the story of Joash. He did as the LORD commanded for as long as the priest Jehoida was alive. However, after Jehoida died, Joash turned away from the one true God towards false idols and even killed Jehoida's son who was also a priest.

Was Jehosheba's rescue then a waste of time? No. Remember she was doing what was right. She was doing God's will. And in the end this rescue was not just about the little boy who became king, it was about rescuing a family line for another baby boy and another king. For a child would be born in the city of David one day – a Saviour – Christ the Lord. The King of kings.

Jehosheba was used by God so that his Son was born as a descendant of King David - just as God the Father planned.

Read more. Find out about Jesus' family tree by reading Matthew 1:1-17 and Luke 3:23-38.

QUEEN OF SHEBA: WISDOM AND WONDER

The story of this great princess once again begins with the story of a great king ... King Solomon. He was the son of King David and ruled over the land of Israel at a time when it was relatively peaceful and prosperous. He had a reputation for great wisdom and wealth. Many wonderful gifts made their way to the doors of King Solomon's palace. Monarchs and leaders from neighbouring countries did their best to cement friendships and alliances with this great leader.

One particular royal lady heard the story of wise King Solomon and was determined to see him for herself. The Queen of Sheba arrived at Solomon's palace with gifts. So here's a question for you. If you were planning an important state visit to a great ruler, what gifts would you bring him? Would you bring ...

a) Large treasure chests of precious stones, all glittery and gorgeous?

b) Mounds of gold, expensive and very heavy?

c) Spices and questions?

What answer did you choose? Do you think you chose the same gift as the Queen of Sheba? I wonder what the Queen of Sheba brought King

Solomon as a gift? Well, that was a trick question really, because she brought all of these things: precious stones, gold, spices and questions. So everyone goes to the top of the class today.

Are you a bit confused about the spices? Well, I can understand that. When you think of spices you probably think of little glass bottles your mum or dad shake into a curry recipe. But spices were very important in Solomon's day. The spices that the Queen of Sheba brought would have been the very best that money could buy. And the Bible tells us that, 'Never again were so many spices brought as those the Queen of Sheba gave to Solomon.' They were very special gifts and greatly sought after.

However, the Queen of Sheba had come prepared with something as well as gifts – she'd come with questions. She knew Solomon was wise. She'd heard the stories and had probably been planning this expedition to Solomon's kingdom for quite some time. It wouldn't have been an easy journey. They would have crossed deserts and climbed mountains. There would have been forests and rivers too. Perhaps, as they rested in their tents at night after the long journey, the Queen of Sheba would have asked some of her courtiers to tell her more about Solomon and his kingdom.

Imagine the queen lying back on her pillows, the stars shining in the night sky. She turns to one of her maidservants and asks for a story of the great king they are going to visit.

'I have heard, oh Queen,' begins one young woman, 'that King Solomon has been given wisdom by God himself and has very great insight. They say he has a breadth of understanding as measureless as the sand on the seashore.

'He is, as you know, the son of the great King David. David will go down in history as a great warrior. Who knows what his son will go down in history as? But he is already known for his wisdom and for the glorious place of worship – the temple – that he has built for the God of Israel.'

The Queen of Sheba shifts herself so that she can look the young girl in the eye. She has many questions to ask this wise and remarkable king but she is puzzled about one thing in particular. 'How is it that Solomon was given wisdom by God?'

'He asked for it,' the maid replies.

'He asked for it?' The Queen of Sheba is astonished.

'Yes, let me tell you the story.' The young girl smiles.

'King Solomon had not long been the King of Israel when God spoke to him in a dream and said, "Ask for whatever you want me to give you."

'Solomon answered, "You have shown great kindness to my father David because he was faithful to you and righteous and upright in heart. You have, my LORD God, made me king in place of my father, David, but I am only a little child and do not know how to carry out my duties. I am here among your chosen people – a great people too many to count. So please give me a wise heart to govern them. May I know the difference between right and wrong."

'God was pleased with what Solomon asked for, so he said to him, "Since you have asked for wisdom and not for long life or wealth for yourself, nor the death of your enemies, but for wisdom, I will do what you have asked. I will give you a wise heart and I will give you what you have not asked for – both wealth and honour. In your lifetime there will not be a king equal to you. If you obey me and keep my commands as David your father did, I will give you a long life."

'Well,' the queen declares, 'God has answered his request. We have heard of this great wisdom. Tell me that story again about the two women.'

The maid nods her head. This is certainly a story that shows Solomon's wisdom at its best.

'One day two women came to stand before the king and one of them said, "Pardon me, my Lord. This woman and I live in the same house, and I had a baby while she was there with me. The third day after my child was born, this woman also had a baby. We were alone; there was no one else there. During the night this woman's son died. She had turned over in her sleep and smothered him. She got up in the night, saw her dead child, and took my living son from my side while I slept. She put her dead son beside me. The next morning I got up to feed my child and he was dead! But I looked at him closely and saw that it wasn't the son that I had given birth to."

'The other woman said, "No. That's not true, Lord King. The living one is my son and the dead one belongs to her."

'The first woman insisted, "No, the dead one is yours and the living one is mine." And so they went on arguing in the very face of the king.

'Solomon then ordered a soldier to fetch a sword. "Cut the child in two and give half to one woman and half to the other."

'The woman whose son it really was, became deeply moved out of love for her child and pleaded with the king, "Please, my Lord, give her the living baby. Don't kill him!"

'But the other said, "Neither I nor you shall have him. Cut him in two!"

'Then Solomon gave his ruling, "Give the living baby to the first woman. Do not kill him; she is his mother."'

The Queen of Sheba lays her head down to sleep. 'What wisdom! What a king! He truly is without equal. We travelled a long way to visit Solomon', she mutters as her maids cover her with a blanket, 'but it has been said that the whole world seeks audience with him just to hear the wisdom that God has put in his heart. His wisdom is greater than all the people of the East, even greater than all the wisdom of Egypt.'

61

'Yes, my queen,' whispers the young maid as she settles herself down to keep watch over her mistress through the night.

When they arrive in Jerusalem the Queen of Sheba makes quite an entrance. The large quantity of spices, precious stones and gold are carried into the city on the backs of camels. Solomon answers all the Queen of Sheba's questions. Nothing is too hard for him to explain. When the queen sees all the wisdom of Solomon and the palace he has built, the food on his table, the officials, servants and cupbearers, as well as the burnt offerings that he makes at the temple of the LORD, she is overwhelmed.

'The report that I heard in my own country about your achievements and your wisdom is true. But I did not believe it until I saw it with my own eyes. Indeed, the truth that I heard was only half of it. Your wisdom and wealth is far greater than the report I heard. How happy your people must be! How happy your servants must be who stand before you and hear your wisdom. Praise be to the Lord your God, who has delighted in you and placed you on the throne of Israel. Because of the Lord's eternal love for Israel, he has made you king to maintain justice and righteousness.'

Read the story of the Queen of Sheba in 1 Kings 10.

PRiNceSS TiPS

The Queen of Sheba wouldn't have wasted her time with Solomon by asking foolish questions. The best questions to ask are about God. The Queen of Sheba must have been asking that kind of questions. In her final speech to King Solomon she said, 'Praise be to the Lord your God, who has delighted in you and placed you on the throne of Israel. Because of the Lord's eternal love for Israel, he has made you king to maintain justice and righteousness.' Here she shows that she knows that God is powerful and that his love is eternal. Follow her example and ask questions about God. Remember you can ask God questions when you pray. He gives you his answers in his Word.

Think about Jesus

In Matthew 12:42 and Luke 11:31 the Queen of Sheba is given another name – the Queen of the South. Jesus said, 'The Queen of the South will rise at the judgment with the people of this generation and condemn them, for she came from the ends of the earth to listen to Solomon's wisdom and now a greater than Solomon is here.'

In this verse, Jesus is talking about himself. He is the king who is greater than Solomon. He is the Son of God. But many people who saw his miracles and heard his message, ignored the truth that Jesus was God's Son. It's the same today. Many people who have access to the Bible and who hear the truth about God, just ignore it.

Jesus tells us in Luke 11:31 that at the day of judgment those people who ignore the wisdom of Jesus will be condemned. On the last day those who have not trusted in God will face punishment for their sins. The Queen of Sheba will be like a witness in a court room. She was willing to travel from the ends of the earth to listen to the wisdom of Solomon and Jesus Christ is far greater than Solomon. We should be willing to do our utmost to learn and follow the wisdom of the King of kings – Jesus Christ.

Read more. Look up the following verses and you'll discover more about prayer: Philippians 4:6; 1 Thessalonians 5:17, Ephesians 6:18; Romans 8:26; Romans 12:12.

eStheR:
The Right Place at
the Right Time

hat is your beauty routine? How much time do you spend in front of the bathroom mirror?

a) Minutes? One look in the mirror, a squirt of this or that and then you brush your teeth.

b) Hours? Well, you have to straighten those curls or curl those straights.

c) Days? Deciding what to wear is just sooo difficult.

d) Months? What? Surely not. Does anyone ever take that long to get beautiful?

Well if you chose answer d) – then you're the same as Esther. Yes, really! Esther's job was to look as beautiful as she possibly could. This was actually quite difficult, even for someone as stunning as she was. She had to use so many cosmetics, it took her twelve whole months to complete her beauty routine. She also had to have special baths for six whole months.

Read on to discover why Esther had to do this. You'll find that the story of Esther is less about perfume and make-up and more about a woman being in the right place at the right time.

The story starts with Esther's people, the Jews. Some time before Esther was born, a great many people had been killed in her home country of

Judah and still others had been taken as slaves to the land of Babylon. Over time those Jewish people who had been exiled from their own country settled in Babylon and began to make their homes there. The country was also called Persia and consisted of 127 provinces that stretched from India to Cush, which is the upper Nile region of Egypt. The ruler at the time of Esther was King Xerxes. And one day this king decided to invite the rulers of the provinces to attend a banquet. He was keen to show off his great wealth and majesty.

King Xerxes and his visiting dignitaries sat down to a feast that lasted seven days. Anyone could come, from the least to the greatest in the capital city of Susa. The garden was decorated with hangings of white and blue linen. The cords were tied to silver rings that were attached to great marble pillars. Gold and silver couches were placed on a mosaic pavement of marble, mother of pearl and other costly stones.

Every guest had his own wine goblet and each goblet was different from the next. There was no limit on the amount of wine that the guests could drink. All the wine stewards were commanded by the king to serve each man exactly what he wished.

At the same time, King Xerxes' wife, Queen Vashti, was giving a banquet for the women. When the last day of the banquet arrived, Xerxes was in high spirits. His banquet had gone well. But he thought it could be better. Xerxes quickly summoned seven of his chief servants and told them to fetch Queen Vashti. 'She is to wear her royal crown and come before me and my guests to display her beauty.'

Vashti was indeed lovely to look at, but when the servants delivered the king's command, Queen Vashti refused to come. The king was furious and burned with anger. Nobody refused the king; no one dared to. Yet his own wife had turned up her nose at his order. Xerxes summoned his wise men to consult them about what should be done with Vashti.

All of the men who came to advise King Xerxes were experts in matters of law and justice. Memukan, one of the chief advisers, replied, 'Queen Vashti has done wrong, not only against the king, but against all the people of this great land. The queen's conduct must surely become known to all women and they will despise their husbands and say, "King Xerxes commanded Queen Vashti to be brought before him, but she would not come." So all the Persian women who have heard what Vashti has done, will respond in the same way. There will be no end of disrespect and discord.'

But what was to be done? Memukan continued, 'If it pleases the king, issue a decree across all the provinces that cannot be repealed. Vashti is never to enter the king's presence again. Let the king give her royal position to someone else who is better. Then when the decree is issued across the land, all the women will respect their husbands, from the least to the greatest.'

The king was pleased with this advice and did as his adviser proposed. But it wasn't long after Vashti had been banished, that the king let his thoughts drift back to the one who had once been his wife. So the king's personal attendants suggested that he began the search for a new queen. Commissioners were appointed in every province to bring all their beautiful young women to Susa. They were to be placed under the care of the king's servant, Hegai. He was in charge of all the palace women and decided what beauty treatments each girl required. All the young women would be presented to the king after the treatments had been completed. The woman who pleased him best would be crowned queen instead of Vashti. As this plan pleased Xerxes, notices containing the king's commands were sent out across the land.

Now, in the city of Susa at that time there was a Jewish man from the tribe of Benjamin. His name was Mordecai. He had a young orphan cousin named Esther that he looked after. She was remarkably beautiful. That was why she found herself being taken to the king's palace and put under the care of Hegai. He saw her potential and immediately provided her with beauty treatments and special food. Esther was given seven female servants selected from the king's palace and she was moved into the best rooms in the women's quarters. But it was a whole year or more before she would be presented to the king. In that year, she would spend many days being covered in oil, myrrh, perfumes and cosmetics.

Before she was even taken to the palace, her cousin, Mordecai, gave her strict instructions. 'Don't tell anyone about your nationality or your family background. If people find out you are a Jewess you could be in danger. I will walk back and forth near the courtyard each day in order to find out how you are and what is happening to you.'

When Esther visited the king he was attracted to her more than to any of the other women. He set a royal crown on her head and made her queen instead of Vashti. Then he gave another great banquet in Esther's honour and a holiday was declared throughout all Susa. It was the beginning of an amazing life for Esther, but it was a life full of danger and intrigue. For a start there were enemies about.

One of the king's nobles, Haman, was a very proud and haughty man. There was a mean streak in him. He insisted that all the people bowed down to him as he passed. Mordecai was the only one who dared to refuse him. Haman wanted him dead, but he decided that he wouldn't waste his energy on killing just one Jewish man. He would kill all the Jewish people in the whole kingdom.

Haman cunningly passed on an ill report of the Jewish people to King Xerxes. 'There is a certain people in your kingdom, sire, that do not follow your laws; it is not in your interest to tolerate them. If it pleases the king, let a decree be issued to destroy them. If this is done, I will give ten thousand pieces of silver to your treasury.'

The king agreed and told Haman to keep the money. 'Do what you like with those people,' he ordered. Haman immediately sent out decrees to all the provinces, that on the thirteenth day of the month the Persians called Adar, the Jewish people were to be massacred. In twelve months time, all the Jewish people were to be killed on a single day.

How strange then that, at this same time, a Jew saved the king's life, and that Jew was Mordecai.

You see, he was still keeping an eye out for his young cousin and often sat at the palace gates in order to get some news. On one of those occasions, he overheard a plot to kill the king. Immediately he sent word to Esther, who in turn, reported it to Xerxes, giving the credit to Mordecai. The incident was recorded in the court records. However, when Mordecai heard that the king had decreed that all the Jewish people were to be killed, he wept loudly. He was so distressed he tore his clothes and put on sackcloth and ashes to show how miserable he was. Esther's servants heard about Mordecai's behaviour and came and told her. She immediately sent him some fresh clothes to wear instead of the sackcloth. But Mordecai would not put them on.

Esther then summoned one of the king's servants to find out what was troubling Mordecai. Mordecai sent the servant back to Esther with a copy of the king's decree. 'Explain this to her and tell the queen that she must go to the king to beg for mercy. She must plead with him for the lives of the Jewish people.'

Esther sent the servant back with the reply, 'If any man or woman approaches the king in the inner court without being summoned, they will be put to death. Unless the king extends the gold sceptre to them and spares their lives, they will be killed. It has been thirty days since I was called to go to the king.'

Mordecai replied, 'Do not think that because you are in the king's house you alone, of all the Jews, will escape. For if you remain silent at this time, deliverance for the Jewish people will arise from another place, but you and your father's family will perish. Who knows, you may have come to your royal position for such a time as this?'

Esther then instructed Mordecai to gather all the Jewish people in Susa to fast for her. 'Do not eat or drink for three days. I and my servants will do the same. When this is done I will go to the king – and if I perish, I perish.'

On the third day, Esther presented herself in

the inner court before the king. He looked at her and was pleased to see her. Xerxes held out the gold sceptre that was in his hand and Esther approached.

Xerxes asked her, 'What is your request? Even up to half the kingdom it will be given you.'

Now comes the surprising bit. Esther didn't ask the king to save the Jewish people; she didn't ask for power in order to change the outcome. Instead, she invited the king and Haman to a banquet.

As they were drinking at the banquet the king asked Esther again if there was anything she wanted. Her reply was the same, 'Let the king and Haman come tomorrow to the banquet I will prepare and then I will answer the king's question.'

Now, Haman thought things were going very well for him. He'd had two invitations from the queen. 'I'm the only person Queen Esther invited to accompany the king to the banquet she is giving,' he congratulated himself. But Haman's good humour vanished as soon as he thought about Mordecai sitting at the palace gates.

At his wife's suggestion, Haman decided to set up a large pole on which he would impale Mordecai. 'Then you can go to the banquet with the king and enjoy yourself,' his wife declared. Haman thought this was a very good plan. But God didn't, and God's plans always prosper.

Do you remember the plot that Mordecai discovered at the palace gates? It had been written up in the court records. That night, King Xerxes couldn't sleep so he asked a servant to get him something to read. The record of the king's reign was brought to him and in it Xerxes discovered how Mordecai had exposed the plot to assassinate him.

'What honour did Mordecai receive for this?' he asked his attendant.

'Nothing has been done for him, my Lord,' the man replied.

Xerxes decided to do something about it. 'Who is in the court?' he asked.

'Haman is there,' the servant said.

'Bring him in,' the king ordered.

When Haman entered, the king asked him, 'What should be done for the man the king delights to honour?'

Now, Haman thought the king was talking about him! So he said, 'Bring him a royal robe and a horse with a royal crest on its head. Then let a royal prince lead this man on the horse through the city streets, proclaiming before him, "This is what is done for the man the king delights to honour."'

'Go at once,' the king commanded, 'and do as you suggested for Mordecai the Jew.'

Haman was horrified, but he had to follow the king's command. After he had led Mordecai through the city streets on horseback, he hurried home. He hadn't long got there, when the king's servants arrived and ushered him away to the second banquet that Esther had prepared. That was when the king, once again, asked Esther what it was that she wanted.

Esther's reply sent chills down Haman's spine. 'If I have found favour with you, Your Majesty, grant me my life and spare my people. For I, and my people, have been sold as slaves only to be destroyed, killed and annihilated.'

Xerxes exclaimed, 'Who is he? Where is the man who has dared to do such a thing?'

Esther replied, 'An adversary and enemy! This vile Haman!'

The king was furious, Haman was terrified. One of the king's servants then let it slip that outside Haman's house was a large pole that he had set up in order to kill Mordecai.

The king ordered that Haman was to be killed on it instead. His property was to be given to Queen Esther and Mordecai was to be welcomed into the presence of the king. As any decree of the king could not be reversed, Xerxes wrote another decree in order to save the Jewish people. Orders were sent to the Jewish people and to all the governors and nobles of the 127 provinces. Jewish people in every city would now be allowed to protect themselves and kill anyone who attacked their families or plundered their properties. On the day that had been chosen to wipe out the

Jewish people in Persia, those who attacked them and those who had plotted to kill them were put to the sword and killed instead.

Read the story of Esther in the Book of Esther chapters 1-10

PRiNceSS TiPS

Esther was ready and willing to put her life on the line for the people of God. She was brave, but she was also obedient. She was the woman that God chose to be in a certain place at a certain time. If Esther hadn't done the right thing, God would have chosen someone else to deliver his people. Sinful human beings can never stop God's plans. When God asks us to do the right thing, it's not because he needs us. He can do anything; he is all powerful. When God uses you as part of his plans it is because it gives him glory and it is a blessing for you and for others.

Think about Jesus

Esther was in the right place at the right time and was used by God to save her people, the Jews. Jesus was in a certain place at a certain time and he was there as part of God's plan to save his people across the world.

God planned Jesus' birth before the world began. He planned that his Son would be born as a baby in a little town called Bethlehem.

God planned Jesus' death before the world began. He knew that his Son would suffer greatly and that it would be his death, the shedding of his blood, that would purchase forgiveness of sins.

Esther could have been replaced. Jesus is the only Son and the only way of salvation. There could never have been any replacement for him. There was no plan B.

Esther saved her people by speaking up for them before the king. Jesus saved his people by taking their punishment on himself, a punishment that they deserved and he didn't.

Esther persuaded King Xerxes to allow the Jewish people to fight for themselves.

Jesus died on the cross – he did all the rescuing that was needed. We don't have to do anything to save ourselves from sin. Jesus has done it all.

He said on the cross, 'It is finished.'

And that's true.

'Believe in the Lord Jesus and you will be saved' (Acts 16:31)

Read more: Look up these verses to find out about Jesus' birth and his arrest: Matthew 1:18 – 2:23; Mark 14:1 – 15:15.

Michal: Secret agent

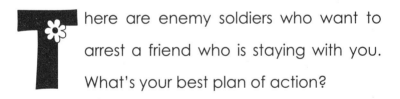here are enemy soldiers who want to arrest a friend who is staying with you. What's your best plan of action?

a) Tell them, 'Let's play hide and seek. Count to 100 and then shout, 'Coming ready or not.'

b) Invent the world's first invisibility potion and pour it all over you and your friend.

c) Take the guards into the house and just show them your guest, sick in bed, 'It's very infectious you know. Cough, cough.'

Did you answer a)? What if the soldiers go, 'One, two, miss-a-few, ninety-nine, one hundred?' You might not have time to hide.

Was it b)? Are you for real? An invisibility potion? How much fantasy fiction have you been reading? Here's a clue – it's fiction – it's fantasy fiction – that means it's not true.

If you answered c) ... you're a devious little diva – are you sure you're not a spy in real life? Answer c) in this instance is pretty much what our Bible princess did on this occasion.

Her name was Michal and she was a younger daughter of King Saul. She was the first wife of David. Saul gave Michal to David as a reward for him killing the Philistine giant, Goliath, and many other Philistine warriors in battle. But Saul had another reason for giving his youngest daughter to David as a wife. He didn't like this young man who was the people's hero. Saul thought Michal would spy on David for him. However, he forgot about that wonderful little word that can cause all kinds of havoc in stories like this – four little letters for a very big emotion: *L o v e*.

Michal loved David and wasn't about to let her father get his nasty little fingers on him.

However, Saul was determined to get the better of David. He didn't care that his daughter was head over heels in love. The fact that David was getting all the attention, made Saul feel sick in his stomach.

Saul even instructed his son, Jonathan, and all the servants to kill David. However, Michal wasn't the only one in Saul's family to support her husband. Jonathan was David's loyal friend. He warned David about his father's plans. 'Saul is looking for a chance to kill you. Be on your guard tomorrow morning. You should go into hiding and then I'll speak to my father about you and find out what his plans really are.'

When Jonathan and his father met the next day, Jonathan spoke well of David. 'Your Majesty, don't do wrong to David; he has not wronged you. He has been a great help to you. He risked his life for you when he killed Goliath and God won a great victory for all of Israel. You saw this yourself and it made you glad. Why then would you harm an innocent man like David, by killing him for no reason?'

Saul listened to Jonathan and promised that David would not be put to death. But before very long, things between David and Saul became bad again.

Because Saul had turned away from the LORD God, God judged him by sending a harmful spirit on him. Saul was moody and depressed one moment and behaved like a mad man the next. While he was in one of his moody moods, it was decided that David should play some peaceful music to soothe his spirits. However, while David was playing the harp, Saul threw a spear at him. David jumped out of the way just in time and then ran home to Michal as fast as he could.

That night Saul sent soldiers to guard David's house. 'Wait until morning,' they were told, 'then go in and kill him.' Michal got wind of this plot and told David what her father was planning. 'If you don't run for your life tonight, tomorrow you will be killed,' she said anxiously.

Between them they worked out David's escape. Michal let David down through a window. It must have been one that the soldiers weren't watching. When David got to ground level he fled. But Michal was still in the house. She needed to give David time to get as far away as possible. This crafty princess devised a rather clever plot of her own.

She took a large statue that was lying about the house and laid it out in David's bed. Quickly, she took some clothes and covered the statue with them. Then she came across a clump of goat's hair. It was just perfect for putting on the head of the statue. In the dim morning light the

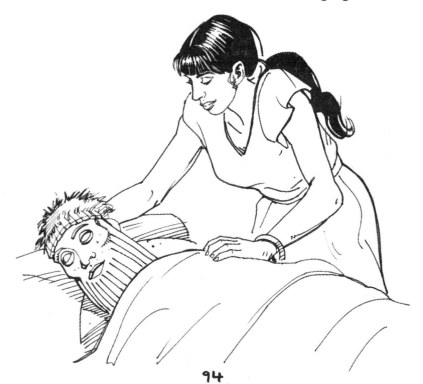

goat's hair, clothes and statue could easily be mistaken for someone sleeping.

When the soldiers arrived the next morning to kill David, Michal told them, 'He isn't feeling well. He's ill.'

I don't understand why they didn't attack the statue thinking it was David, but they didn't. They went back to Saul to tell him that David was feeling poorly. Saul was annoyed. 'Bring him up to me in his bed so that I may kill him.'

That was when they discovered that they'd been duped by Michal. They walked up to the bed and discovered a great big statue, some old clothes and a bunch of goat's hair. They must have felt stupid.

Now Michal had to face the wrath of her father. But again she was ready for whatever came her way.

'Why did you deceive me like this and let my enemy escape?' Saul thundered.

Michal told him, 'He said to me, "Let me get away."'

Now, she knew, and we know, that David said no such thing. Lying is not something that God wants you to do. In fact, read the Ten Commandments, God tells us not to lie. But this was Michal doing her own thing, working out her own plot.

She should have realised that it wasn't her cunning or bravery that would save David; it was the LORD God.

Michal was clever and brave and stood up to her father, but it was the one true God who planned everything. It was his power and might that delivered David and protected Michal. It was certainly not Michal's brains and definitely not her lies.

Some time later, after Saul's death, Michal showed her true colours. When the ark of the LORD was returned from captivity David and all of Israel rejoiced greatly.

Now, just in case you don't know, the ark of the LORD was a special chest that was kept in the temple. It had been captured by the Philistines, but had given them so much trouble, they sent it back. That is why the people of Israel were celebrating. And David was in the middle of it all.

David discarded his royal robes and began to dance in a simple linen tunic. It wasn't what a king usually wore. David danced before the LORD with all his might, while he and all Israel brought up the ark of the LORD with the sound of trumpets.

Michal watched David dancing from inside a window. And when she saw King David leaping and dancing before the LORD, she despised him in her heart.

After David had finished sacrificing burnt offerings, he blessed the people in the name of the LORD Almighty and all the people went to their homes. Then Michal came out to meet her husband and said, scornfully, 'How the king of Israel has distinguished himself today, going around half-naked in full view of the slave girls of his servants as any vulgar fellow would!'

David said to Michal, 'I was dancing before the LORD, who chose me rather than your father when he appointed me ruler over the LORD's people Israel. I will celebrate before the LORD. I will become even more undignified than this, and I will be humiliated in my own eyes. But by these slave girls you spoke of, I will be held in honour.'

I think the ending to this story is a bit sad. How much better it would have been for Michal if she had come and worshipped the LORD God with her husband, giving God the glory for keeping her and David safe. But instead of being a true Bible princess she let her pride get the better of her. She looked at her husband and despised him for doing something beautiful. She despised her husband for praising God.

Read the story of Michal in 1 Samuel chapters 18 and 19; 2 Samuel chapter 6.

PRiNCeSS TiPS

What we can learn from the life of Michal is that a woman should never despise her husband. She should always support him when he is worshipping the Lord. She should follow his lead and praise God and give glory to him.

It's not a good sign when you plan things without praying to God for guidance. Michal's actions were clever and brave, but she did not seek God's instruction. When she lied to her father we can see that she was really just doing things in her own way. Make sure that you take your plans and hopes to God in prayer. Ask him to guide you and to protect you. Ask him to deliver you from temptation.

Think about Jesus

The word 'despise' is horrible. Isn't it dreadful to think of a wife despising her husband for doing something that is good and right? How disappointed David must have been to see the woman he cared for treating him like that.

Jesus knows what it is like to be despised by others. The prophet Isaiah described what it would be like for God's Son – hundreds of years before Jesus was born. Isaiah prophesied about the suffering that the Saviour would experience.

'He was despised and rejected by mankind, a man of suffering, and familiar with pain. Like one from whom people hide their faces he was despised, and we held him in low esteem' Isaiah 53:3.

The soldiers who crucified Jesus put a crown of thorns on his head and mocked him. When Jesus was dying on the cross one of the criminals yelled at him, 'You say you're the Messiah – save yourself and us!'

Even Jesus' closest friends rejected him and betrayed him. You may shake your head and say, 'How could they do that to Jesus?' but if you have not recognised the fact that you are a sinner and need Jesus as your Saviour, then you're no different. If you haven't asked God for his forgiveness and trusted in Jesus to save you from your sin, you too are despising Jesus.

There is no middle ground with God. You are either for him or against him. Do not reject Jesus. He died on the cross and was raised to life again. He deserves great glory for this.

Read more about Jesus' death and resurrection:
Luke 22:31 – 23:56; John 20:1 – 21:25

JeZeBeL: Bad PRinCeSS 1

ere's a question for you. You are a princess, but you are married to a king who is a cry baby. He really wants something that belongs to someone else. He wants it so much but, he can't get it, as he goes to his bed in a sulk. What would you do to sort out the situation?

a) Ignore his bad mood – he'll get over it.

b) Organise a party and get everyone to bring him a present.

c) Plot and scheme a dastardly wicked plan to get the king what he wants – it will involve murder, so it's really bad.

Any normal woman would pick a). That's what usually happens when someone gets the sulks. They snap out of it sooner or later.

Any normal princess would probably pick b) – she can afford it.

But the bad princess we're being introduced to this time chose c) and her name was Jezebel. Her name has gone down in history for all the wrong reasons. She is the perfect example of what a wicked woman is. All Jezebel was good for was plotting, scheming and painting her face.

Jezebel's plot came into being because her husband, King Ahab, had seen a vineyard that he really wanted. It belonged to a man called Naboth and it was close to Ahab's palace at Jezreel. Ahab asked Naboth to sell the vineyard to him, but Naboth was not willing. The land had been passed down to him through the generations. Naboth didn't want to sell it for anything.

Ahab was miserable. He went home, lay on his bed and sulked. He even refused to eat.

When Jezebel saw this, she asked, 'Why are you so sullen? Why won't you eat?'

Ahab answered, and I imagine he sounded like a great big baby when he said this, 'I said to Naboth the Jezreelite, "Sell me your vineyard; or let me give you another vineyard in its place." But he said, "I will not give you my vineyard."'

Jezebel replied, 'Is this how you act as king over Israel? Get up and eat! Cheer up. I'll get you the vineyard of Naboth the Jezreelite.'

So she wrote letters in Ahab's name, placed his seal on them, and sent them to the nobles who lived in Naboth's city. In those letters she wrote: 'Gather the people together and seat Naboth in a prominent place. But put two scoundrels opposite him. They are to accuse him of cursing God and the king. Then take him out and stone him to death.'

That is exactly what happened.

As soon as Jezebel heard that Naboth was dead, she said to Ahab, 'Get up and take possession of the vineyard of Naboth the Jezreelite. He is no longer alive, but dead.'

Ahab's sulk vanished and he got up and went down to take possession of the vineyard.

Ahab and Jezebel must have thought they had got away with it. The nobles and scoundrels would be too scared to say anything. Nobody else would be able to disclose what had really happened. But there is One who sees everything. Ahab and Jezebel had forgotten about God.

The word of the LORD came to the prophet Elijah: 'Go down to meet King Ahab. He has gone to take possession of Naboth's vineyard. Say to him, "This is what the LORD says: Have you not murdered a man and seized his property? In the place where dogs licked up Naboth's blood, dogs will lick up your blood—yes, yours!"'

When Elijah approached the king, Ahab turned to him and said, 'So you have found me, my enemy!'

'I have found you,' Elijah answered, 'because you have sold yourself to do evil in the eyes of the LORD. The LORD says, "I am going to bring disaster on you. I will wipe out your descendants because you have aroused my anger."'

Elijah also prophesied that Jezebel would die by the walls of Jezreel and that dogs would eat her up.

All of Elijah's prophesies came true. Ahab died in battle and, as they cleaned his chariot at a pool in Samaria, dogs came and licked up his blood that dripped onto the ground. Jezebel also died just as God had told Elijah she would. One day, as she was putting on her eye make-up, and arranging her hair. she looked out of her window and saw Jehu. He had just been anointed as King of Israel instead of her son, Joram. Jehu, the LORD's anointed king had, in fact, just killed Jezebel's son with a shot to the heart.

As Jehu entered the gate, Jezebel asked, 'Have you come in peace you murderer of your master?'

Jehu then looked up at the window and called out, 'Who is on my side? Who?'

Jezebel's servants looked down at him. 'Throw her down!' Jehu said. So they threw her down. Jezebel died at the walls of Jezreel just as Elijah had said. There was nothing left of her to bury in the end. What a terrible death for someone who was a king's daughter.

Read about Jezebel in 1 Kings chapters 18 to 21.

PRiNCeSS TiPS

The Bible says that, 'There was never anyone like Ahab, who sold himself to do evil in the eyes of the LORD, urged on by Jezebel, his wife.' To urge someone else to go against the LORD means that you are sinning yourself and you are leading someone else into sin. This is something you should not do.

The story of Naboth's vineyard is very sad. How terrible for his family to see Naboth being falsely accused and then stoned to death. It all happened because one greedy king wanted something that belonged to someone else. This is called coveting. Perhaps you think coveting is a small sin and not that wicked. You're wrong. God tells us in his commandments not to covet.

It is often at the root of other sins. In the story of Naboth's vineyard, coveting is at the root of the sin of lying, stealing and murder.

Think about Jesus

Naboth was falsely accused and then unjustly put to death. Jesus knows what that is like. When he was put on trial the chief priests arranged for men to testify falsely against him. He was then taken outside the city to be crucified. This was unjust, but it was far worse than Naboth's death because this was the Son of God who was being killed. He had not done even one sin that deserved God's anger, yet here he was being punished by sinful men. However, it was all part of God the Father's plan. He had to punish his perfect Son in order to save sinners from the punishment they deserved. The blood of Jesus had to be shed in order for God's anger to be turned away from the sinners who deserved it. Religious leaders and Roman soldiers nailed Jesus to a cross, but when he died, he died because it was part of God's plan and he was willing for this to happen.

Read more. Look up the following verses. They will show you what God was doing before he made the world – John 17:24; Ephesians 1:4; 1 Peter 1:20.

HeRoDiaS' DaUGHteR: BaD PRiNCeSS 2

magine you are a beautiful dancing princess. You've had some very expensive lessons and you know all the right moves. You're asked by the king to dance at one of his banquets. You do such a good job of it that he says, 'I'll give you anything you want – even half of my kingdom.' What would you do?

Would you say ...

a) Yes please. Half of your kingdom would do very nicely.

b) That's very kind of you, but I'll settle for half of your gold and jewels.

c) Hmmm ... I don't know ... can I just go and ask my mum?

If you answered a) – well, I think that's a very good answer don't you? After all, he suggested it.

If you answered b) – well, that might be an even better answer. Running a country means an awful lot of work. Jewels and money are a lot less hassle.

If you answered c) - there's no way you're a princess? What's your mum going to say to you? If she's got any sense she'll say, 'Ask for the kingdom and I'll rule it for you. Then I'll give you the jewels too.'

But in this story the princess did go and ask her mum. Now why did she do that? Let's find out.

The Bible doesn't give us this princess's name, but a lot of people think she was called Salome. The king she was dancing before, was King Herod – not the Herod who wanted to kill Jesus as a child, but one of his descendants. He was a vicious ruler and inside his palace prison he had John the Baptist in chains.

Herod could have had him executed but he didn't. There was something about John that made him nervous. Herod knew that John was a righteous and holy man. He also knew that the people really respected John as a prophet, so Herod was worried about making the people angry by killing him. But Herod couldn't release John because his wife, Herodias, hated the man.

You see, John the Baptist had told Herod and Herodias that their relationship was sinful. Herodias had been married to someone else and now she was married to Herod. What they were doing was wrong and John the Baptist told them that. Herodias didn't like anyone to tell her she was wrong. She let her hatred simmer away inside her until a certain opportunity for murder arose. It all took place on Herod's birthday.

Enter: the dancing princess.

She was a good dancer, a very good dancer. She didn't let nerves get the better of her.

She danced for all the guests and pleased Herod so much that he promised to give her whatever she asked. 'Even half my kingdom,' he exclaimed. The princess went to consult with her mother who told her to ask for 'the head of John the Baptist on a plate.'

When Herod heard that, he was distressed, but because of the promise he had made in front of his dinner guests, he granted her request. John was beheaded in the prison and his head was brought in on a platter and given to the girl, who carried it to her mother.

You can read about Herodias in Matthew 14.

PRINCESS TIPS

Once again, this particular princess is not one you should try and be like, but her story is in the Bible for a reason. We don't know if the young princess listened to John the Baptist's preaching, but she definitely listened to her mother who was quite the wrong person to listen to. Just as you shouldn't lead others into sin, you shouldn't let others lead you into sin. Whatever you are asked to do, it doesn't matter who is doing the asking, if it is against God's Word you should not do it. Always stand up for the truth.

Think about Jesus

It is important to think about Jesus, to find out about him and who he is. John the Baptist did this. When he heard about all the miracles that

Jesus was doing, he told two of his disciples to go to Jesus and ask him, 'Are you the one who is to come, or should we expect someone else?'

John wanted to know for sure if Jesus was the Saviour that God had promised. Jesus replied to the messengers, 'Go back and tell John what you have seen and heard: The blind receive sight, the lame walk, those who have leprosy are cleansed, the deaf hear, the dead are raised, and the good news is proclaimed to the poor.'

All these things that Jesus mentioned showed his power – he had power over sickness and disease, even death – but the greatest thing he had power over was sin. The good news of the gospel was being preached. Jesus could save the body and he could also save the soul. He was indeed God's Son, the promised Messiah.

Read more about Jesus' power: Mark 10:45-47; Luke 8:40-42; Mark 4:38-40; Luke 5:5-7.

So What about You?

You may not be a princess, but are you a child of God? Think about this verse from Psalm 45. It was written for a princess on her wedding day.

Listen, daughter, and pay careful attention: Forget your people and your father's house. Let the king be enthralled by your beauty; honour him, for he is your lord.

But quite often in the Bible words that have been written for one situation have been written for something else as well – there's a double meaning. This verse was not just written for a princess long ago; it was also written for men and women who trust in the Lord Jesus as their Saviour.

God is telling you, if you are a Christian, that he is to be the most important person in your life. He is to be more important than friends and family. You are to live a life that honours God because

he is your Lord and King. When God looks on you, he wants to be pleased with you. He wants you to remind him of his Son, Jesus Christ.

When you put God first, you will find that your love for friends and family grows. When you love God most, you will love your family even more than you do now.

In Proverbs 31, God describes what a really wise woman is like. She speaks with wisdom and faithful instruction is on her tongue.

We've found out quite a bit about wisdom by going through the lives of these princesses from the Bible. We've read about the wise things they said and did and we've read about some who did foolish and evil things too. The princesses of the Bible have taught us that it's not being a princess that's important, it's being a child of God. It's not about being born into a royal family, it's about trusting in God and being part of his

heavenly family. Princesses may be important, but God is the ruler of all the earth. Jesus Christ is the King of kings and the Lord of lords.

Do your actions and words show others that you love God? Do you, like the woman in Proverbs 31, speak with wisdom? Beautiful princesses can be seen in glossy magazines. They look amazing and everyone thinks they are wonderful. But as the Bible says, 'Charm is deceptive and beauty is fleeting.' A princess and her good looks don't last forever. The clothes and the glitter all pass away. But God's Word does not pass away and a woman who loves God and his Word is to be praised. She is worth more than rubies and she is worth more than princesses who wear rubies. She is worth this because of her great God – and he is worthy!

Read more: Look up Proverbs 31 to find out more about the wise woman who is worth more than rubies.

Who is
Catherine Mackenzie?

I live in the Highlands of Scotland, in a town called Inverness. I have loads of nieces and nephews and some of them have red hair like me. As a young girl, I was an avid reader and I still am. The only way my parents could persuade me to take my medicine was to 'bribe' me with a book.

When I grew up a little, I remember being allowed to read in bed for an extra half hour and thinking it was the best thing ever.

In school, I loved to write stories in class, though my spelling was more than a bit wobbly. However, that wasn't the worst mistake I made at that age. It took some time for me to realise that I was a sinner and that I needed Jesus to save me.

I thought I was good enough for God. I wasn't. When I became an older teen, I realised that the Lord Jesus died to save me from my sin.

That was when I found something life-changing to write about – the Word of God; Jesus Christ; Salvation – the topics are endless.

I started by writing articles for our church newspaper and finally wrote my first book when I was in my twenties. I was asked to write a biography about a man called Richard Wurmbrand. And since then, writing true life stories has been a major part of my life.

The main reason I write, is because there is a wonderful true life story that has given my life real meaning – the life, death and resurrection of my Lord Jesus Christ. Of all the heroes and heroines I've written about, he is the best.

Books Ablaze

...and other historical stories
you've got to hear

Irene Howat

Sniff, sniff ... am I smelling burning? No, it's not dinner - there are some bonfires in this book.

Books were amongst some of the things set alight during church history. In fact, flames were used to persecute Christians throughout church history.

Their possessions and homes were set alight. Christians were even killed and burned for their faith.

Irene Howat tells the Christian story behind some amazing historical incidents. You will see how not even fire, or the plans of evil men, can separate Christians from the love of God.

ISBN: 978-1-84550-781-7

On Fire

...and other Bible stories
you've got to hear

Irene Howat

Watch out – these stories are H...H...H...Hot! Each one is about fire – but there's not a matchstick or a marshmallow in sight! They are all from the Bible and show how God has used fire throughout Scripture in a variety of ways.

He used fire to get Moses to pay attention and to help the Israelites find their way through the dark. Jesus himself cooks a fish barbie on the beach after his resurrection and the Holy Spirit comes down on the disciples at Pentecost with tongues of flame.

ISBN: 978-1-84550-780-0

CHRISTIAN FOCUS PUBLICATIONS

Christian Christian CF4K Mentor
Focus Heritage

Christian Focus Publications publishes books for adults and children under its four main imprints: Christian Focus, CF4K, Mentor and Christian Heritage. Our books reflect that God's Word is reliable and Jesus is the way to know him, and live for ever with him.

Our children's publication list includes a Sunday school curriculum that covers pre-school to early teens; puzzle and activity books. We also publish personal and family devotional titles, biographies and inspirational stories that children will love.

If you are looking for quality Bible teaching for children then we have an excellent range of Bible story and age specific theological books.

From pre-school to teenage fiction, we have it covered!

Find us at our web page:
www.christianfocus.com

CF4·K
Because you're never
too young to know Jesus